Searchlight
BOOKS™

Do You Dig
Earth Science?

Studying

Soil

Sally M. Walker

Lerner Publications Company
Minneapolis

Lerner Publications Company
A division of Lerner Publishing Group, Inc.
241 First Avenue North
Minneapolis, MN 55401 U.S.A.

Website address: www.lernerbooks.com

Library of Congress Cataloging-in-Publication Data

Walker, Sally M.
      Studying soil / by Sally M. Walker.
          p.   cm. — (Searchlight books™—Do you dig earth science?)
      Includes index.
      ISBN 978–1–4677–0023–8 (lib. bdg. : alk. paper)
      1. Soils—Juvenile literature. I. Title.
      S591.3.W353 2013
      577.5'7—dc23   2012022475

Manufactured in the United States of America
1 – PC – 12/31/12

Contents

Chapter 1

WHAT IS SOIL?

Did you ever make mud pies when you were little? If you did, soil was one of the ingredients you used. You may have called it dirt instead of soil.

This field has good soil. A farmer will grow plants in the soil. What are some other places where soil can be found?

Where Is Soil?

Soil is in lots of places. You can find soil under the grass. It surrounds tree and flower roots. It lies beneath sidewalks and streets. If you could lift your home, you would probably find soil under it too!

Tree roots grow deep into the soil.

What's in Soil?

A scoop of soil contains many things. Soil has rocks in it. Plants and bits of leaves are in soil. Many creatures live in soil too.

You can be a soil detective. See what you can find in the soil near your home. You will need a shovel. Ask an adult where you may dig. Use your shovel to dig out several handfuls of soil. Look closely at your soil. What can you find in it?

IF YOU LOOK CLOSELY AT SOIL, YOU MAY FIND WORMS, INSECTS, OR OTHER ANIMALS LIVING IN IT.

Soil is a natural resource. Natural resources are materials found on Earth that help living things. They are made by nature, not people. Soil helps plants and animals grow. They cannot live without it. But where does soil come from?

These plants need soil to grow.

Chapter 2

HOW SOIL FORMS

Soil is made up of different kinds of materials. One of these materials is bits of rock. Rocks are broken pieces of bedrock. Bedrock is the layer of solid rock that covers the outside of Earth.

Hard rocks can break into small pieces. How can water break rocks?

As water rushes down this hill, it breaks off bits of rock.

Wind, Water, and Ice

Rocks are hard. But they can be broken into tiny bits. Tiny bits are called particles. Wind, water, and ice are strong enough to break rocks.

Wind blows sand grains against big rocks. The sand grains scrub off particles of rock.

Rushing water in rivers makes rocks roll and tumble. The rocks break into smaller pieces. Tiny particles of rock break loose.

Rainwater seeps into cracks in rocks. If it gets cold enough, the water freezes. It becomes ice. Ice takes up more space than water. So the ice pushes against the rock. It makes the cracks bigger. Pieces of rock break off.

Ice split this huge rock in half.

Glaciers are giant, moving slabs of ice. Glaciers are very heavy. Their weight slowly grinds big rocks into small pieces.

Minerals

Rocks are made of minerals. A mineral is a hard substance made in nature. Minerals are not alive, like plants or animals. The minerals in a rock become part of the soil when the rock breaks apart.

Minerals add nutrients to soil. Nutrients are substances that help living things grow. Soil contains nutrients that plants and animals need to stay healthy.

This glacier carries rocks with it as it flows.

Humus and Bacteria

Humus is the second material that is in soil. Humus is dark brown or black. It is made of bits of dead plants and animals.

Humus is made by bacteria. Bacteria are tiny living things. They are so tiny that they can be seen only with a microscope. Microscopes are tools that make small things look big.

Bacteria are turning these dead leaves into humus.

There are many kinds of bacteria. They live nearly everywhere on Earth. This picture shows one kind of bacteria that lives in soil.

Bacteria eat dead plants and animals. They break the plants and animals into tiny pieces. The pieces become humus. Humus contains nutrients that had been inside the plants and animals. The nutrients can become part of the soil.

Air

Air is the third material in soil. Soil is full of air spaces. Some air spaces are large. You can easily see them. You can see the tunnels that earthworms dig in soil. An earthworm's hole is filled with air. Soil also has tiny air spaces. The tiny spaces are between bits of minerals and humus. Most of these spaces are too small for you to see. But they are there.

As earthworms move through the soil, they make tunnels.

Put a handful of marbles or small rocks in a jar. Can you see spaces between the marbles or rocks? Air fills these spaces. Now imagine that you can shrink the marbles or rocks. Imagine making them as tiny as the smallest particles in soil. The air spaces would still be there. They would just be much smaller.

AIR FILLS THE SPACES BETWEEN THESE ROCKS.

Water

Water is the fourth material found in soil. Water can move around in soil. It trickles through the soil's air spaces. The moving water picks up nutrients from the soil. The water carries the nutrients into the roots of plants.

Water has filled the air spaces in this soil.

Water also carries tiny particles of soil into the big air spaces. Put a handful of soil on top of the marbles or rocks in your jar. Pour in a small glass of water. Where does the water go? What happens to the particles of soil?

When you pour water on the soil, the water flows down between the rocks. The water carries bits of soil with it.

Where Soil Forms

Soil forms on flat land. It forms alongside rivers. It forms on forest floors and on low hills. Soil forms as humus and rock particles begin to pile up. It can take hundreds of years for 1 inch (2.5 centimeters) of soil to form.

Deep soil has formed on this flat land.

Soil cannot form in some places. Soil cannot form on steep mountains. That's because soil-making materials slide down the mountain. Soil cannot form in very windy places or places where water flows quickly. In these places, soil-making materials can't pile up. They do not have enough time to become soil.

Soil can't form on the steep sides of this mountain.

Chapter 3

LAYERS OF SOIL

If you dig deep down into the ground, you may notice different colors of soil. These are different layers of soil. A layer is a single thickness of soil. A blanket lying on your bed is a layer. A cake may have several layers. Soil has layers too.

We usually see only the top of the soil. What is this soil layer mostly made of?

Horizons

A soil layer is called a horizon. The horizon that is closest to the surface is called the A horizon. This layer is made mostly of humus. The A horizon has many nutrients. It helps plants grow.

This soil is made mostly of humus. It is full of nutrients that growing plants need.

Under the A horizon is the B horizon. The B horizon has less humus. It has more sand and small rocks.

You can see different layers in this soil.

The C horizon is the deepest soil layer. It is just above the bedrock. The soil in the C horizon has lots of big, chunky rocks. The A and B horizons cover the C horizon. They protect the C horizon from water, ice, and wind.

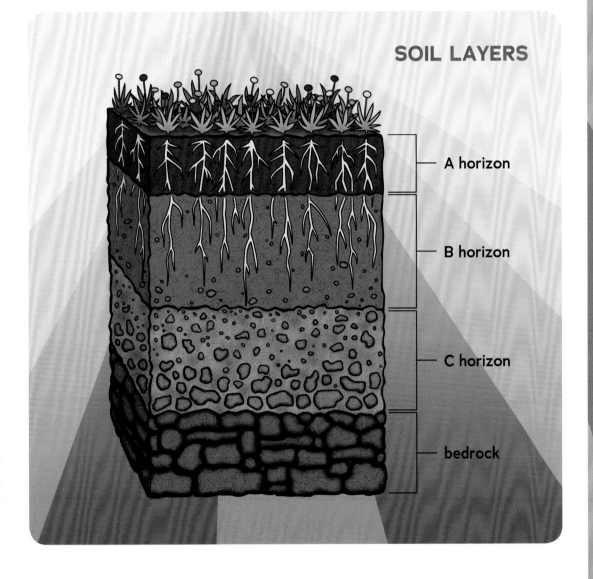

SOIL LAYERS

A horizon

B horizon

C horizon

bedrock

Chapter 4

WHAT SOIL LOOKS LIKE

Soil can be made of many different kinds of minerals. Different minerals can be different colors. The minerals and humus in soil help give the soil its color. Many soils are a shade of brown. But some are yellow. Some are even bright orange red.

Most soils are brownish. But some are other colors, such as red. What gives soil its color?

Textures and Particles

Soil also has different textures. Texture is how rough or smooth something is. The texture of soil depends on the size of the soil's particles.

The largest mineral particles in soil are called sand. You can see the mineral particles in sandy soil. Sand particles feel rough when you rub them between your fingers. Some sand-sized particles have sharp, jagged edges. Others are mostly round.

Some of these sand grains have sharp edges. Others are smoother.

Another kind of particle in soil is called silt. Silt particles are much smaller than sand particles. It's hard to see silt particles. If you rub silt between your fingers, it feels smooth. Silt-sized particles are shaped like sand particles.

Clay particles are the smallest particles in soil. They are too small to see without a microscope. Clay particles are flat.

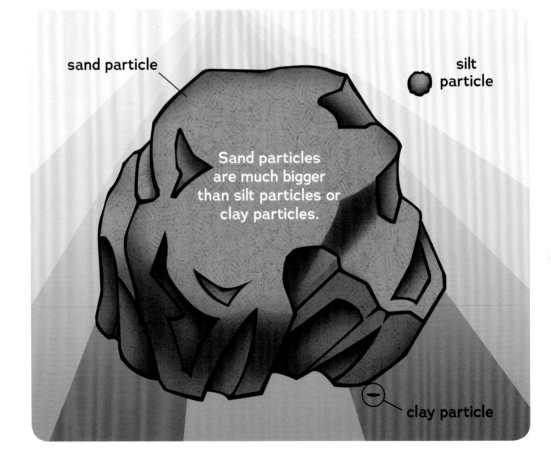

sand particle

silt particle

Sand particles are much bigger than silt particles or clay particles.

clay particle

Sand particles have big air spaces between them. Water drains quickly through the spaces. So puddles rarely form in sandy soil. Silt particles have smaller spaces between them. Water takes longer to drain through small spaces.

Water drains quickly through sand. That's why you don't usually see many puddles on sand at the beach.

Flat clay particles get squeezed together. The spaces between clay particles are tiny. Water has a hard time trickling through tiny air spaces. Clay particles also soak up water. So it takes a long time for water to drain through soil that has a lot of clay.

Water drains slowly through clay particles. When it rains, puddles often form in soil that has many clay particles.

Loam

Soil with equal amounts of sand, silt, and clay particles is called loam. Loam is very good for growing plants. It holds just the right amount of water for growing roots.

Soil that has mostly sand-sized particles is called sandy loam. Water drains quickly through sandy loam. Soil with mostly clay-sized particles is called clay loam. Water drains slowly through clay loam. Rain often forms puddles in clay loam.

This picture shows sandy soil (LEFT), loam (CENTER), and clay soil (RIGHT).

What Is Your Soil Like?

What kind of texture does your soil have? Rub the soil between your fingers. Does it feel rough, smooth, or in-between?

DIFFERENT SOILS HAVE
DIFFERENT TEXTURES.

When wet clay loam dries out, it breaks into hard chunks.

Put some soil in your palm. Add a small amount of water to your soil. Add only enough to make the soil moist. If it seems too wet, add a little more soil. Mix the soil and water together with your fingers. See if you can mold the soil into a flat circle. If you can, your soil has a lot of clay. If the circle crumbles, the soil contains more sand and silt than clay.

Chapter 5

TAKING CARE OF SOIL

Soil is a very important natural resource. It takes a long time for soil to form. So we must take good care of Earth's soil.

We need soil so trees and other plants can grow. What happens when people spray chemicals outside?

Hurting Soil

People often use chemicals to kill harmful bugs or weeds. Some of these chemicals may stay in the soil. The chemicals can hurt animals, people, and other plants. So people must be careful not to use too much of these chemicals.

Farmers often spray chemicals on their fields.

THIS PLACE WAS ONCE A FOREST. PEOPLE CUT DOWN MOST OF THE TREES. RAIN HAS WASHED AWAY A LOT OF THE SOIL.

Tree roots help hold soil in place. Cutting down too many trees leaves the soil unprotected. Then water and wind can sweep the soil away.

Farmers plant crops in soil. A crop is a kind of plant, such as corn or wheat.

Different kinds of crops are growing on this farm.

Conserving Soil

A farmer can damage soil by planting the same crop in the same field year after year. The crop uses up the soil's nutrients. After a while, plants can no longer grow in that field. Wise farmers conserve soil. Conserving soil means using it wisely. Growing different crops every few years keeps a field's soil healthy. Then the field can be used for a longer time.

Farmers also conserve soil by plowing their fields the right way. Plowing is breaking up the soil. Plowing makes grooves in the soil so crops can be planted in rows. If the grooves go straight down a hill, rain can easily wash soil away. Instead, the farmer can make grooves that circle around the hill. Then the grooves make ridges of soil. The ridges stop rain from flowing down the hill. The soil stays in place.

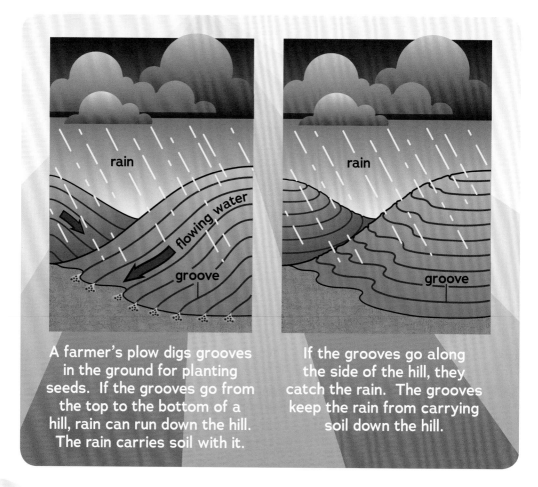

A farmer's plow digs grooves in the ground for planting seeds. If the grooves go from the top to the bottom of a hill, rain can run down the hill. The rain carries soil with it.

If the grooves go along the side of the hill, they catch the rain. The grooves keep the rain from carrying soil down the hill.

Soil in Your Life

The next time you go outside, look at the soil around you. Notice its color. See what kinds of plants are growing in it. Feel its texture.

Watch how people take care of the soil. Try to think of ways that you can care for the soil around your home. Plants, animals, and people will always need healthy soil!

Taking care of the soil is important.

Glossary

bacteria: tiny living things that can be seen only with a microscope

bedrock: the layer of solid rock that covers the outside of Earth

clay: the smallest mineral particles in soil

conserve: to keep something from being lost or wasted

glacier: a giant, moving slab of ice. Glaciers form in places that are cold all year long.

horizon: a layer of soil

humus: a dark brown or black substance that is a part of soil. Humus is made of bits of dead plants and animals.

loam: soil that has equal amounts of sand, silt, and clay particles. Loam is very good for growing plants.

mineral: a hard substance found in nature. A mineral is not alive.

natural resource: a material found on Earth that helps living things. It is made by nature, not people.

nutrient: a substance that helps living things grow

particle: a very small piece of something

sand: the largest mineral particles in soil

silt: medium-sized mineral particles in soil. Silt particles are smaller than sand particles but larger than clay particles.

texture: the roughness or smoothness of an object

Learn More about Soil

Books

Gardner, Robert. *Super Science Projects about Earth's Soil and Water*. Berkeley Heights, NJ: Enslow, 2008. Complete these science projects to see how soil and water are connected.

Lindbo, David L., Wendy Greenberg, Laurel Hartley, John Havlin, Thomas E. Loynachan, Monday Mbila, and Bianca Mobieus. *Soil!: Get the Inside Scoop*. Madison, WI: Soil Science Society of America, 2008. Learn about different types of soil, soil's purposes, and why soil is so important to all living things.

Montgomery, Heather L. *How Is Soil Made?* St. Catharines, Ontario: Crabtree Publishing, 2010. This book will teach you about the parts of soil, nutrients, and how weathering and erosion work.

Riley, Joelle. *Examining Erosion*. Minneapolis: Lerner Publications Company, 2013. Discover the basics of erosion, including what causes erosion, how landforms and soil change over time, and what we can learn from observing the forces of nature at work.

Websites

Discovery Education: The Dirt on Soil
http://school.discoveryeducation.com/schooladventures/soil
Learn about the layers of soil and some of the creatures that live there. Then go on an underground adventure!

Growing the Next Generation
http://www.growingthenextgeneration.com/just-for-kids.html
Watch videos, play games, and explore recipes to find out about soil, plants, nutrients, and more.

TLC: Science Projects for Kids—Soil Experiments
http://tlc.howstuffworks.com/family/science-projects-for-kids-soil-experiments.html
Try these simple science experiments to learn more about soil and plants that grow in it.

Index

Photo Acknowledgments

The images in this book are used with the permission of: © Royalty-Free/CORBIS, pp. 4, 6, 21; © Mark Schneider/Visuals Unlimited, Inc., p. 5; © Photodisc/Getty Images, pp. 7, 32; © Karlene Schwartz, p. 8; © John R. Kreul/Independent Picture Service, p. 9; © Robert & Jean Pollock/Visuals Unlimited, Inc., p. 10; © John Freeman/Lonely Planet Images/Getty Images, p. 11; © Basement Stock/Alamy, p. 12; © Dr. Dennis Kunkel/Visuals Unlimited, Inc., p. 13; © Nigel Cattlin/Photo Researchers, Inc., p. 14; © Todd Strand/Independent Picture Service, pp. 15, 17 (both); © Nigel Cattlin/Alamy, p. 16; © Gilbert Twiest/Visuals Unlimited, Inc., p. 18; © Marli Miller/Visuals Unlimited, Inc., p. 19; © Franois De Heel/Garden Picture Library/Getty Images, p. 20; © Lancia Klein/Vetta/Getty Images, p. 22; © Laura Westlund/Independent Picture Service, pp. 23, 26, 36; © Tom Edwards/Visuals Unlimited, Inc., p. 24; © Scimat/Photo Researchers, Inc., p. 25; © Science Faction/SuperStock, p. 27; © age fotostock/SuperStock, p. 28; © Wally Eberhart/Visuals Unlimited, Inc., p. 29; © iStockphoto.com/Julija Sapic, p. 30; © Dave Reede/All Canada Photos/SuperStock, p. 31; © iStockphoto.com/David H. Lewis, p. 33; © Mark Boulton/Photo Researchers, Inc., p. 34; © Georg Gerster/Photo Researchers, Inc., p. 35; © iStockphoto.com/Svetlana Foote, p. 37. Front cover: © iStockphoto.com/Igor Stramyk.

Main body text set in Adrianna Regular 14/20
Typeface provided by Chank

VESTIGATES NA
S NATIONAL GEOGRAPHIC
GEOGRAPHIC INVESTIGAT
C INVESTIGATES NATIONA
TES NATIONAL GEOGRAPH
L GEOGRAPHIC INVESTIG
HIC INVESTIGATES NATIO
GATES NATIONAL GEOGRA
NAL GEOGRAPHIC INVEST
PHIC INVESTIGATES NATI
TIGATES NATIONAL GEOG
IONAL GEOGRAPHIC INVE
RAPHIC INVESTIGATES N
ESTIGATES NATIONAL GE
NATIONAL GEOGRAPHIC I
EOGRAPHIC INVESTIGATE
INVESTIGATES NATIONAL

Ancient
Greece

Archaeology Unlocks the
Secrets of Greece's Past

Ancient
Greece

Archaeology Unlocks the Secrets of Greece's Past

By Marni McGee

Michael Shanks, Consultant

NATIONAL
GEOGRAPHIC

Washington, DC

Contents

< Casts of marble heads found in the ruins of Aphrodisias, a Greco-Roman city that
flourished in modern Turkey beginning in the second century B.C.

‹ The remains of Hadrian's Gate at Ephesus. The most important Greek city in Asia Minor, Ephesus was later taken over by the Romans.

What happened in ancient Greece has captured people's imagination for hundreds of years. Some see the ancient Greeks as the direct ancestors of the Western world because they seem to

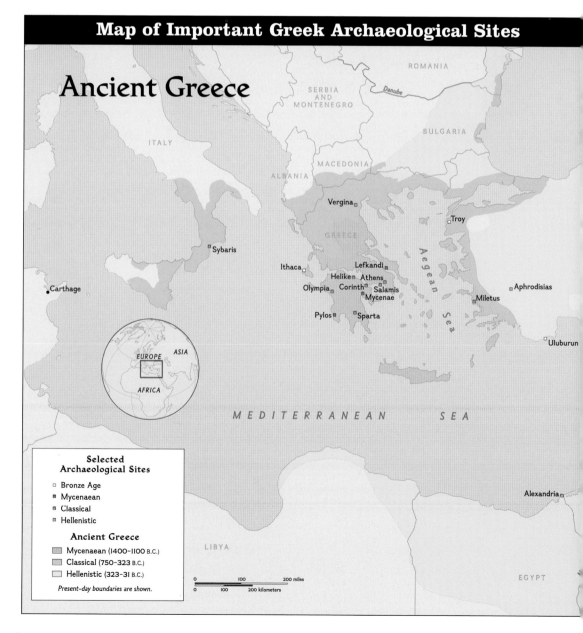

Map of Important Greek Archaeological Sites

Ancient Greece

ROMANIA

SERBIA AND MONTENEGRO

Danube

BULGARIA

ITALY

MACEDONIA

ALBANIA

Vergina

GREECE

Troy

Sybaris

Ithaca

Lefkandi

Helike Athens

Olympia Corinth Salamis

Mycenae

Carthage

Aphrodisias

Miletus

Pylos Sparta

Aegean Sea

Uluburun

EUROPE ASIA

AFRICA

MEDITERRANEAN SEA

Selected Archaeological Sites

- □ Bronze Age
- ▪ Mycenaean
- ▫ Classical
- ▫ Hellenistic

Ancient Greece

- Mycenaean (1400–1100 B.C.)
- Classical (750–323 B.C.)
- Hellenistic (323–31 B.C.)

Present-day boundaries are shown.

Alexandria

LIBYA

0   100   200 miles
0 100 200 kilometers

EGYPT

have invented so much of what the modern world holds most dear—great learning, art, science, and even the way we organize ourselves in democratic society. We know about the ancient Greeks because they wrote about themselves, but also because archaeologists explore what is left of their world: the ruins and remains of their cities, the buildings, tombs, shipwrecks, rich treasures, and everyday objects. What is fascinating about archaeology is not so much the story of the past it reveals, although that can inspire us. What really captures our imagination are the stories of how we can all connect with the wonders of the past: stories of underwater discovery, scientific excavation, finding long-lost palaces and investigating their remains. This book can start you off on these amazing journeys of exploration.

∧ Michael Shanks studies his notes on a field trip to Olympia.

Michael Shanks

Professor of Classical Archaeology, Stanford University

FOUR MAJOR
Ages of Greece

Mycenae

ca 1400—1100 B.C.

In the Late Bronze Age the city of Mycenae in the Peloponnese was a dominant power in the Aegean Sea. Its citadel was said by Homer to be the seat of Agamemnon, who led the Greeks in the Trojan War. Mycenae was prosperous and traded by sea with Egypt, Syria, and Palestine. Its merchants kept records in an early form of Greek. In about 1100 B.C. the city's power ended when it was attacked and burned by unknown invaders.

Dark Age

ca 1100—750 B.C.

After the fall of Mycenae, writing was lost: the term "Dark Age" refers to the lack of historical records rather than a lack of achievement. It used to be thought that new peoples moved into the Aegean from the north. Kings emerged to rule small local communities. These were the forerunners of Greek city-states. Poets began to record myths and legends, which were written down in the 8th century B.C., when Greek speakers began writing again, using a version of the Phoenician alphabet.

< The "House of the Warrior" vase was found in the citadel at Mycenae. It was made around the 12th century B.C.

Timeline of Greek History

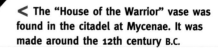

1000 B.C.	750	500	250	B.C. o A.D.	250	500

ca 1400 B.C. Mycenaean civilization begins

ca 1250 B.C. Trojan War

ca 1100 B.C. "Dark Age" begins

ca 776 B.C. First Olympic Games

ca 700 B.C. Homer writes *Iliad* and *Odyssey*

ca 700 B.C. Rise of city-states

461 B.C. Pericles begins Golden Age of Athens

331 B.C. Alexander the Great defeats Persia

86 B.C. Athens conquered by Rome

404 B.C. Sparta and its allies defeat Athens after 27-year Peloponnesian War

A.D. 306 Constantinople becomes capital of Byzantine Empire

476 Fall of Rome

◀ Mycenae

| Dark Age | Classical Age | Hellenistic Period |

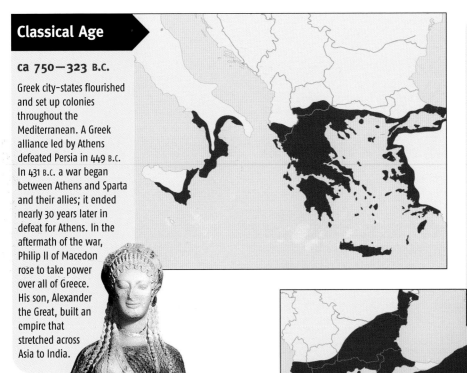

Classical Age

ca 750–323 B.C.

Greek city-states flourished and set up colonies throughout the Mediterranean. A Greek alliance led by Athens defeated Persia in 449 B.C. In 431 B.C. a war began between Athens and Sparta and their allies; it ended nearly 30 years later in defeat for Athens. In the aftermath of the war, Philip II of Macedon rose to take power over all of Greece. His son, Alexander the Great, built an empire that stretched across Asia to India.

ca 323–31 B.C.

Although Alexander's empire broke into three major and many smaller territories, Greek influence lived on in Hellenistic–Greek–politics, literature, art, and language, encouraged by education and widespread use of writing. The Romans moved into Alexander's former territory in 168 B.C. and in 86 B.C. captured Athens. The Romans proved enthusiastic supporters of many aspects of Greek culture.

Hellenistic Period

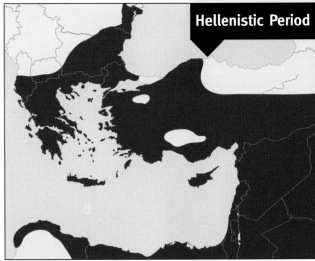

< This statue of a young woman—known as a *kore*—was made in the Dodecanese region of Greece in the sixth century B.C.

750   1000   1250   1500   1750   A.D. 2000

800s Byzantium expands control throughout Greece

1204 Crusaders sack Constantinople

1453 Ottomans capture Constantinople

1823 Greek independence

1974 Greece becomes a republic

Yesterday Comes Alive

How do we learn what we know about the past?

Archaeologist George F. Bass is fascinated by the Bronze Age in Greece. As a young man, he took diving lessons in the pool at the YMCA so that he could explore the wreck of a ship in the Aegean Sea near Turkey. Bass later helped found the Institute of Nautical Archaeology (INA) to run underwater excavations around the world, including the Aegean. He became known as the "father of nautical archaeology."

< George F. Bass measures part of an underwater site while a photographer records the process.

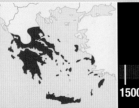

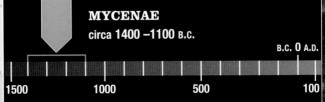

MYCENAE
circa 1400 –1100 B.C.

B.C. 0 A.D.

1500   1000   500   100

A New Wreck

In 1983, the INA learned of another find in the Aegean, near the town of Uluburun in Turkey. A diver had found hunks of metal on the seabed. He said they looked like "cookies with ears." INA divers soon established that the hunks of metal were part of the cargo of a ship that had sunk centuries earlier. A huge amount of other cargo lay nearby.

In the summer of 1984 George Bass and his team of underwater archaeologists strapped on scuba gear and flippers and began to explore the wreck. The work was hard because the cargo lay more than 150 feet (45 m) below the surface. Excavators could dive for only 20 minutes, twice a day. Longer dives could cause "the bends," a dangerous, even fatal, sickness.

Sunken Treasure

The dive team could see that the ship was old, but no one dreamed how old—or how valuable—until they began to study the cargo. They carefully measured and photographed everything. An archaeological site is

▽ Divers lift a large amphora, or storage jar, from the seabed. It may have been used to hold fresh water for the voyage.

< George Bass examines a bowl from the Uluburun wreck. This one came from Cyprus—but much of the cargo came from other places, creating a puzzle about where the ship originally sailed from.

∨ The archaeologists used wooden poles to build a rickety-looking expedition headquarters on the rocky headland overlooking the wreck site.

like a crime scene: Nothing should be moved until experts have recorded not only what they found but also where they found it. Once the objects had been recorded, the divers lifted them to the surface, where they could be cleaned and examined more closely.

Among the hundreds of objects the divers found, one had a vital clue about the age of the wreck. It was a beetle-shaped charm called a *scarab*. Scarabs were common finds—people carried them for luck. But this one was special: It bore the engraved symbol of Nefertiti, a 14th-century B.C. Egyptian queen. The scarab was so valuable it probably belonged to the ship's captain or a wealthy merchant onboard. It helped date the wreck to around the queen's lifetime. The ship offered Bass a unique glimpse into the Late Bronze Age of ancient Greece.

Homer's Heroes

Archaeologists, historians, and scholars of literature have long been fascinated by the Greek Bronze Age, a time made famous by its heroes.

< Golden chalices and pottery amphorae lie as they were found. For the divers, the jumbled wreckage became a huge puzzle.

down. How much was added in the retelling? How much left out? Finds like the Uluburun wreck help archaeologists to discover how accurate Homer's stories really are.

The Oldest "Book"

In the *Iliad*, for example, Homer mentions a folded writing tablet. But the earliest tablets archaeologists had ever found dated from the eighth century B.C., six hundred years after the Trojan War! Experts assumed that such details must have been added to the poems later—until one of Bass's divers made a remarkable discovery.

Amid the wreckage on the seabed lay a writing tablet with an ivory hinge—the oldest known "book" in the world. The wooden tablet had once been coated with beeswax. The writer would have used a pointed stylus to scratch words into the wax. The wax had gone, so we will never know what message it carried, or what language the message was in. But Homer had been right—making archaeologists think again about the history of writing in Greece, which had begun earlier than they thought.

Testing the Sources

Greece is one of the best known of all ancient civilizations. The Greeks had many stories about themselves, many

Nearly three thousand years ago the poet Homer wrote his epic poems, the *Iliad* and the *Odyssey*, describing the adventures of Greek heroes during a war between the Greeks and the city of Troy, in modern-day Turkey.

Homer's long poems offer glimpses of daily life, but they also contain fantastic details, like quarreling gods and a princess who hatches from an egg. For years, scholars believed that Homer made up his stories, even though they reflect a real war that had been fought hundreds of years before he lived. Stories about the Trojan War and its heroes were told and retold for centuries before they were written

of which were later written down. Archaeology in Greece often involves checking written accounts against the physical evidence—and vice versa.

At Uluburun, for example, Bass found a hundred jars of resin from the terebinth tree. A scholar named Victor Loret believed that the resin was burned in religious ceremonies by the ancient Egyptians, who imported tons of it by ship. But Loret had no proof, and very little terebinth resin had ever been found. Loret's theory depended on the meaning of the Egyptian word *sntr* (pronounced "sonter"), which one scholar believed meant "pistachio nut." Bass realized that the jars in the wreck were similar to jars shown in

< Air-filled balloons lift artifacts to the surface that are too heavy for divers to lift.

∧ The oldest-known "book" in the world has two carved wooden panels joined by ivory hinges.

△ A reconstruction of a Bronze Age ship: its cargo is based on the finds at Uluburun, but the deck is based on a 14th-century Egyptian tomb painting.

Egyptian tomb paintings. In the paintings, the jars were labeled "sntr." Loret was right—and Bass's discovery not only helped to reveal the meaning of an Egyptian word. It also showed that the early Greeks might have burned terebinth resin in their religious rituals, as the Egyptians did.

Everyday Clues

The Uluburun wreck yielded a huge number of finds. Some were valuable, such as ivory from hippopotamus tusks, a gold cup, amber beads, and silver jewelry from Egypt and Canaan. Other finds were more practical—but just as valuable as archaeological clues. Swords, bows and arrows, and curved knives suggested that the Aegean was perilous for sailors, who likely carried them to defend the ship against pirates. Kitchen pots and bowls contained traces of the sailors' diet: seeds, almonds, raisins, and figs. There were 24 stone anchors: Only a very

large ship sailing in dangerous waters would have needed so many.

The "cookies with ears" turned out to be blocks of copper and tin that could be melted together to make bronze. After more than 22,000 dives over 11 years, the team collected 10 tons of copper and 1 ton of tin— enough to make bronze weapons for a whole army!

Logging In

Even ebony logs from Africa that were being carried in the ship's cargo provided valuable information. The end of a log shows a pattern of rings, each of which marks a year's growth for the tree. The rings vary in thickness, because the tree grows at different speeds every year depending on, for example, the amount of rainfall. By comparing the rings with patterns from other ancient logs, Bass worked out that the ship had sunk in 1316 B.C., more than 33 centuries ago.

On its last voyage, the ship likely sailed from a port in what is now Syria or Israel. Its cargo astonishes scholars.

These ancient sailors were already trading across three continents: Africa, Asia, and Europe!

Tell Us a Story

The Uluburun wreck is one of the latest in a series of discoveries about Bronze Age Greece that began more than 130 years ago with Heinrich Schliemann, a German archaeologist who believed that Homer's Troy was a real place—he just wasn't sure where.

Other people had realized that Troy once stood in Anatolia, in present-day Turkey. After looking for clues in Homer's poems, Schliemann agreed. At Hissarlik, a mound of earth rose 105 feet (32 m) above the coastal plain. In the local language, Hissarlik meant "palace." The clues all fit, and so in 1870, Schliemann started to dig.

Archaeologists call mounds like Hissarlik *tells*. Tells are formed when towns are built and rebuilt over time on the same site. The site becomes like a layer cake. The oldest layers of the settlement are at the bottom, but every layer has its own secrets.

Archaeologists call the layers in a tell *strata*. They dig through each layer

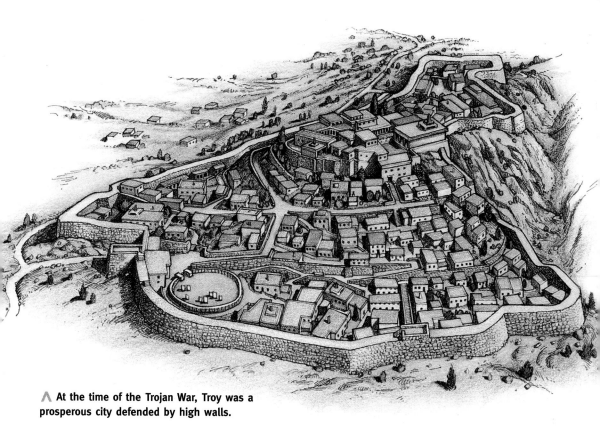

⋀ At the time of the Trojan War, Troy was a prosperous city defended by high walls.

Learning From Layers

Stratigraphy is the study of *strata*, the layers of remains left by different societies on the same site. The layers might contain trash such as animal bones or bits of broken pottery, or rubble from buildings. Today stratigraphy is part of the most basic techniques of archaeology. At the time Schliemann excavated Hissarlik, however, it was still a new approach to digging. Archaeologists were not accustomed to carefully recording what they found at each level of a site. Some modern archaeologists criticize Schliemann for destroying the upper strata at Hissarlik—and the information they contained about Troy's later occupants.

⋀ **Archaeologists at the Greek city of Sinop in Turkey dig through layers of settlement, including the remains of a wall.**

carefully, recording what they find. Schliemann was only interested in Homer's Troy. Even though the tell at Hissarlik had up to 13 layers, he got his workers to dig a deep trench right through the site.

At the bottom of the mound, Schliemann found a settlement about 5,000 years old. He called the city Troy One. In the next layer up, he found bronze weapons and gold jewelry. He named the settlement Troy Two—and announced that he had found Homer's legendary city.

Schliemann had amazed the experts. Some said that he must be wrong. Others complained that he was only after fame. Schliemann certainly did some things that no archaeologist would do today. He cleaned up the jewelry from Troy Two, then got his wife Sophia wear it in photographs later published in the newspapers. Schliemann even took jewelry out of Turkey without the government's permission!

The Hunt for Troy

Today, archaeologists believe that Schliemann found the right site—but the wrong level. In the 1930s, Carl Blegen, an archaeologist from the

University of Cincinnati, discovered that a settlement at a higher level within the mound matched Homer's Troy far better than Troy Two. Troy Six existed in the 13th century B.C., which is when the Trojans battled the Greeks. The city had tall limestone walls, protected gates, and large towers. Burn marks on its stones showed that the city had been destroyed by fire and violence, just as Homer said it was.

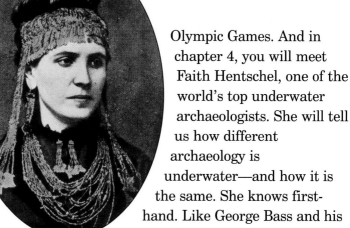

∧ Sophia Schliemann wearing jewelry from Troy. It later disappeared.

Work is still going on at Hissarlik. Archaeologists use scientific instruments like magnetometers and ground-penetrating radar to see into the earth like an x-ray. They no longer have to dig to find remains of the past!

Watery Work

Ever since Schliemann's explorations in 1870, archaeologists have been learning more about Greece's past, including secrets from the time before stories and records were written down. In chapter 2, you'll learn how excavation of ancient ruins is casting light on what was once called the Dark Age. Chapter 3 describes the beginnings of the

Olympic Games. And in chapter 4, you will meet Faith Hentschel, one of the world's top underwater archaeologists. She will tell us how different archaeology is underwater—and how it is the same. She knows first-hand. Like George Bass and his colleagues, Dr. Hentschel had to become an expert diver. These archaeologists use waterproof cameras and special note boards and pencils to record what they find. They must be as careful under the sea as they would be on land.

Chapter 5 takes us back to the ocean floor for a visit to Alexandria, a great Egyptian city now "hiding" at the bottom of the harbor. Finally, in chapter 6, you will read about a few of the most recent discoveries in Greece. Some support the accounts left by ancient writers, but others suggest a new scenario. Greece and the sparkling Aegean still have secrets just waiting to be discovered.

< This lavish gold earring was part of what Schliemann called "Helen's jewels."

Getting the Word Out

When Schliemann announced his discovery of Troy, many scholars said he was more interested in publicity than in finding out about the ancient world. The same criticism has also been aimed at many later archaeologists—and some do make dramatic claims about their discoveries and get their photographs in the press.

In many ways, however, this publicity is vital. Many archaeologists want to share their findings with the public, not just with other experts. They say that even appearing on a TV talk show can encourage people to visit exhibits or sites. They argue that it does not matter how you get people into a museum, as long as they enjoy it when they get there and are interested in what they see. Publicity also helps raise money from governments and universities—excavation and restoration are very expensive!

Schliemann's publicity had lasting results. Today, Troy is one of the most famous archaeological sites in the world. In 2004, the Trojan War was the subject of a Hollywood movie. Experts criticized the film for being inaccurate, but it helped to make Troy familiar to a new generation of viewers.

∧ Orlando Bloom and Diane Kruger star in *Troy*. The film was popular—but also highly inaccurate.

Light in the Darkness

What really happened during the "Dark Age" of Greece?

The leader of the Greeks at Troy was Agamemnon. His fortress of Mycenae was a tremendous stronghold. The walls were so huge that later Greeks thought they must have been built by a race of giants, the one-eyed Cyclops. Goods from Mycenae reached the far ends of the known world, and Mycenaean warriors set the standard for fine armor and weaponry that spread to

< A night-time view of Mycenae from its Lion Gate. The palace that now lies in ruins was said to be home to the legendary king Agamemnon.

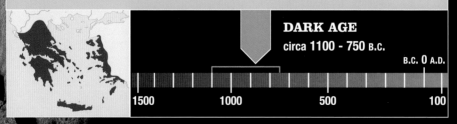

DARK AGE
circa 1100 - 750 B.C.

B.C. 0 A.D.

1500   1000   500   100

western Europe and Scandinavia. But their power did not last. By the 12th century B.C., their fearsome roar had dwindled to a sigh.

The End of Mycenae

What happened? Archaeologists have found other sites in the Aegean that shared the same culture as Mycenae. The ruins all stand on high ridges, where it was easier to fight off attackers. On a high ridge above the modern town of Pylos, Carl Blegen and a team from the University of Cincinnati began to dig on a rainy day in April 1939. The shallow soil soon revealed its secret: the remains of a palace. Large pottery jars still held traces of wine and oil, and the pantries were stocked with bowls and cups. There was a large banqueting room. There was even a bathroom featuring a decorated tub. Such a luxury item surely could only have belonged to a person of wealth and importance.

Blegen concluded that the palace had belonged to King Nestor of Messenia, whom Homer had described in the *Odyssey*. It had almost no fortifications, suggesting that the Messenians were more peaceable than the people of Mycenae. Or perhaps they relied on their warlike neighbors for defense. Like all Greek peoples, the

> Heinrich Schliemann discovered this gold mask at Mycenae and announced that he had looked upon the face of Agamemnon. Modern experts disagree—some even suggest the mask is a fake.

Zooarchaeology

The analysis of animal remains like the bones in Nestor's palace is called *zooarchaeology* or *archaeozoology*. It can be a very important source of information about ancient sites. It tells us what animals people ate or kept as pets. The types of animals are clues about the ancient environment, but they also reveal whether people farmed or hunted their food, and even what sacrifices they made to their gods. Most animal remains that survive are bones or other hard parts such as teeth or horns. They are usually easy to identify, because experts can compare them to living species. Experts can tell how old an animal was

Mules that once turned a mill in an ancient town.

when it died by studying how worn its teeth are. Bones can give clues to any diseases the animal might have suffered. They are also useful because they can be used for radiocarbon dating, a technique that measures the amount of carbon in objects to tell how old they are.

Messenians worshiped the gods of nature. Their land had winding streams, rich valleys, and fertile meadows. Living so close to the ocean, they knew that they had better keep the sea god Poseidon happy.

Bull's-Eye

Archaeologists from the University of Cincinnati returned to Pylos in 1991 to see what else they could learn. In 1996, graduate student Sharon Stocker was surprised to discover large jars full of bones—lots of them—in a storage room. The second surprise was

that the bones had been burned at a very high heat. Stocker and her husband, Professor Jack Davis, thought that they were probably the bones of sheep and goats, but they guessed wrong. An archaeologist who specializes in animal remains identified them as the bones of bulls. Surprise #3!

Homer wrote that when the son of Odysseus visited King Nestor, he found the people of Pylos by the seashore. They were sacrificing black bulls to the gods. The bones of the animals were roasted over open fires.

> This statue of Zeus, the king of the Greek gods, once brandished a thunderbolt.

Dark Days

The Mycenaean civilization collapsed about 1100 B.C. The Mycenaeans moved to the edges of their territory, on outlying islands and coasts. They traded less and practiced a simpler kind of farming, growing only enough food for their families. Their old strongholds fell into ruin.

Archaeologists have found that by the tenth century B.C. about four-fifths of Mycenaean settlements had been abandoned. It used to be thought that new peoples may have arrived in Greece, including the Dorians from the north. The legend is that the Dorians were too poor for fancy dishes or jewelry. They seem not to have known how to read or write, so there are no written records. Some scholars call the years between 1100 and 750 B.C. the Dark Age.

This was exciting news. What Davis and Stocker had found matched the written record exactly. The bones confirmed Homer's account of how the bulls' throats were cut and their blood sprinkled on an altar. Servants wrapped the bulls' thighbones with fat, and priests roasted them over a sacred fire. The ritual aimed to please the gods with delicious food. After the gods were "fed," the king and his guests feasted on roasted meats and wine.

Burn marks on stones show archaeologists that Nestor's palace was destroyed by sudden violence. It burned down around 1200 B.C. What happened? Did warriors attack? No weapons were found in the banquet hall, and no human skeletons were found in the palace, so there may not have been any fighting. Was the king taken with his people as the slaves of their conquerors? No one knows the answers… yet.

Light in the Dark

In 1981, new light began to illuminate the darkness. But it was a close call: British and Greek archaeologists had to rush to save a site at Toumba, near Lefkandi on the island of Euboea. They knew that the hillock contained the ruins of a tenth-century B.C. building. The owner wanted to build on the land, however, and by the time

the archaeologists arrived, a bulldozer had cleared the top 10 feet (3 m) of the mound. About a third of the ancient building was destroyed.

Enough remained to show that the ruined building was very large—135 feet (41 m) long and 30 feet (9 m) wide. It also hid a secret. In a shaft beneath the main room, four horses had been buried with a man and a woman. The man had been cremated and his ashes placed in a bronze vessel. The archaeologists guessed that the woman might have been the man's wife. She may have been sacrificed, because an iron knife still lay beside her skeleton. The whole structure seems to have been built in honor of the dead man, who might have been a king or a heroic warrior. Such tombs were known to have been built later in Greece, but the resting place of the "Hero of Lefkandi" is the earliest ever found.

Buried Treasures

The Lefkandi tomb is only one part of a settlement that had five cemeteries, and there were many other exciting finds in the complex. Objects buried in some of the graves showed that Euboea during the Dark Age was not as isolated or backward as archaeologists had once thought. There were goods from a wide area, including the Greek mainland, the island of Cyprus, and even bronze vases from Egypt. The Euboeans seem to have traded widely and lived well. For them, the Dark Age turns out not to have been so dark after all.

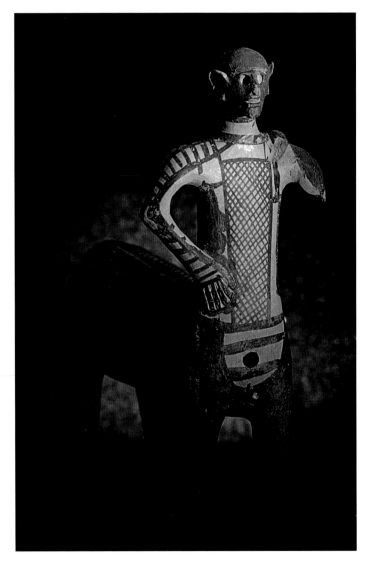

 This terra-cotta statue from Lefkandi dates from the second half of the 10th century B.C.

Greeks on the Move

Why did the Greeks build cities all around the Mediterranean?

Around 800 B.C., the Greeks began trading more widely again. In 776 B.C., runners, jumpers, and wrestlers from 13 cities met at Olympia to honor Zeus, the king of the gods. This was the first Olympic Games. Worshiping Zeus was one of the few things the Greeks agreed on. Even when they were at war with one another, they stopped fighting to hold the games.

‹ When ancient sites sink or silt up, like the ancient port of Miletus in Turkey, archaeologists have to use special techniques to excavate the wet ground.

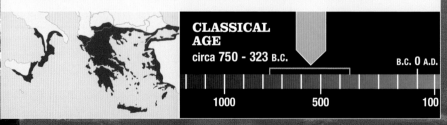

CLASSICAL AGE
circa 750 - 323 B.C.

B.C. 0 A.D.

1000   500   100

In 1958 German archaeologists discovered a very old running track at Olympia, where the earliest games were held. It measures 232 yards (212 meters). According to legend, Hercules paced it out… exactly 600 steps.

Not only Greeks but also Romans, Syrians, Turks, North Africans, and the peoples of Asia Minor honored the early Olympic winners, just as today we admire modern Olympic heroes. Hundreds of vases and statues show ancient athletes crowned with a winner's wreath.

> The Palaistra at Olympia was a covered space where athletes could train during bad weather.

Turning to Trade

As the Greeks once more opened their eyes to the world, they became interested and ambitious again. Small farming communities grew into towns and cities, usually centered around a high, fortified area—called an *acropolis*—where people could seek refuge in times of danger. The cities came to dominate the nearby land, creating what are known as city-states.

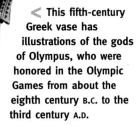

< This fifth-century Greek vase has illustrations of the gods of Olympus, who were honored in the Olympic Games from about the eighth century B.C. to the third century A.D.

Trade flourished. A fifth-century B.C. writer, Hermippos of Athens, describes a typical cargo arriving into the harbor of Athens, which was one of the most important cities in Greece. From his verses, we learn that the Greeks traded their wine and olive oil for almonds, dates, apples, pears, cheeses, meats, wheat flour, and tasty foreign figs they believed would bring sweet dreams. Greek ships also carried ox hides, papyrus from Egypt for making rope, ivory from Africa, and colorful carpets from Carthage.

We may call these traders "businessmen," but many were more like pirates—not so much trading as simply taking what they wanted.

Counting on Colonies

With growing trade and travel, the Greeks established colonies—200 of them in the 200 years between 750 and 550 B.C. Ambitious Greeks looked overseas for adventure and the chance of profit. They sailed for Italy, Spain, Egypt, Syria, North Africa—ports all over the Mediterranean world—and even north into the Black Sea.

Some colonists were forced to leave their homeland. A law, passed in Cyrene—in what is now Libya— decreed the death penalty for anyone who refused an order to sail to the colonies. But the colonies also offered great opportunities. There, the younger sons of aristocrats could become landowners and political leaders, perhaps growing as rich as their older brothers back home. Adventurers of all kinds took up the challenge. Sometimes the colonists merged peacefully with native peoples, but often they seized land by force.

Archaeologists have found Greek pottery, coins, temples, and statues all across Europe, Asia Minor, and northern Africa. These finds show how widely Greek ships traveled—carrying goods, colonists, and ideas to places far from Greece itself.

Soggy Sybaris

One of the most famous Greek colonies was Sybaris, which was widely known for its wealth and the easy lifestyles of its citizens. The word *sybaritic* is still used to describe luxurious living. Sybaris was known

to have stood on the Gulf of Taranto in southern Italy, but when archaeologists began to search for its remains in the 1870s they started an effort that would last for 60 years—and come up with nothing. The site could lie anywhere in an area of about 450 square miles (1,165 sq. km). The land was marshy, and it was almost impossible to dig holes in the wet soil without them collapsing.

The search for Sybaris was abandoned until the 1960s when an Italian team led by Carlo Lerici and a team from the University of Pennsylvania led by Froelich G. Rainey tackled the site with a range of new archaeological tools. They used

∧ A restorer pieces together urns from a Greek colony in Italy.

electronic sound sensors that sent radar signals into the ground. The echoes that came back varied according to what material they bounced off. The archaeologists soon discovered a long wall that they hoped might have belonged to an ancient city,

but instead, it turned out to be an ancient seawall built to protect the coast from flooding.

Stuck in the Mud

The team carried out a survey of the site. They established that, if the ruins of Sybaris lay on the site, they were more than 20 feet (6 m) down—too deep for the electronic sound sensors. Next they tried a survey using a proton magnetometer, which is lowered deep into a bore hole. This instrument measures tiny variations in the earth's magnetic field caused by buried objects or structures such as walls. By digging 850 bore holes and studying fragments they found, Rainey's team established that they had indeed found an ancient city, but it turned out to be Copia, a later town built by the Romans. Sybaris lay deeper still.

A few years later Rainey tried again with a new magnetometer that contained the element cesium. Cesium is so sensitive that the device could reach deeper into the mud. Soon Rainey's team found the foundations of large buildings, which he announced were the remains of Sybaris. The team took photographs from airplanes using infrared scanners that measured tiny variations in the ground's heat. The images allowed them to map the layout of the buried city and choose a site for digging. They pumped water out from the location and dug deep down into the dry mud to uncover part

The Greeks built theaters wherever they started colonies—this one is at Miletus. Some are so well designed that they are still used today, and people in the back seats can hear every word clearly from the stage.

of a Greek theater. Sybaris had been found at last!

Mighty Miletus

One city that founded many colonies was Miletus, which stood in modern-day Turkey on the Meander River. The river's curving path gave us the verb "to meander," meaning to wander around. The site has been excavated by German archaeologists since the 1890s. Work has stopped only during World Wars I and II—but much still remains to be discovered. Miletus was once one of the busiest cities in the Greek world.

Excavators have established that the earliest settlement on the site dated from before 5000 B.C. In the fifth and sixth centuries B.C., it became a thriving port through trade with its colonies around the Mediterranean and the Black Sea. Archaeologists have found the ruins of not one but four harbors. High above the town stood an altar to Poseidon, the god of the sea who protected merchants and sailors.

The citizens of Miletus enjoyed a high standard of living. Excavations have revealed two open-air markets, a large public bath complex, and a theater. The city was taken over by the Romans, but the evidence shows that in the sixth century A.D., the harbors silted up—possibly because of changes in the course of the Meander. The once-mighty Miletus was abandoned.

The City of the Goddess

How did Athens come to dominate Greece?

It's not always easy being an archaeologist in Athens. The city is home to the most famous of ancient Greek sites, and one of the most famous archaeological sites in the world: the Acropolis. The beautiful buildings of the Acropolis, or "heights of the city," perch on a rocky outcrop overlooking the capital. The site is crowded with tourists, and the stones of its buildings have been damaged by pollution from traffic. For hundreds of

< This Greek sculptor took two years to carve this marble column-top as a replacement for the ancient original in the Acropolis in Athens.

CLASSICAL AGE
circa 750 - 323 B.C.

B.C. 0 A.D.

1000   500   100

years its temples and other buildings were neglected or remodeled; they were even blown up. Many beautiful sculptures were removed. Even today the Greeks are still trying to get back some marble carvings taken from the Acropolis by British officials in the first decade of the 19th century.

Holy High Places

The Acropolis was dedicated to the city's gods, especially to Athena. Athena's temple, the Parthenon,

∧ **The Parthenon was badly damaged in 1687. It was being used to store explosives during a war when it was hit by a cannonball and blew up.**

dominates the city skyline. From here, the goddess looked over her city. Around her temple, the sacred walled enclosure contained other temples and buildings. Ancient accounts report that one bronze statue of Athena stood so tall that sailors could see the sunlight glinting off her helmet from 30 miles (48 km) out at sea.

The City of Pericles

In the fifth century B.C., a nobleman named Pericles became the leading figure in Athenian politics. Under his direction, Athens began a building program which included the creation of the Acropolis. This was a huge project, but Athens was rich, thanks to its fleet of wooden ships, or *triremes*. The city became richer still when the other Greek city-states joined Athens in a military alliance and paid Athens to protect them against their common enemies.

American scholars digging in the Acropolis in the 1920s found stone records of payments from as many as 265 other cities. Pericles used the money to rebuild the city, which had been destroyed by the Persians in 480 B.C. He hired the sculptor Phidias to oversee the work.

The Agora

If the Acropolis was the religious center of Athens, the heart of its trade and politics was the *agora*, or marketplace. American scholars began exploring the agora as early as 1929. Five years later, they discovered the ruins of Tholos, a circular building where a committee of citizens managed city business.

Archaeologists from the American School of Classical Studies went on to excavate the whole of the agora. At the end of the 20th century the work was directed by John Camp. He discovered that the sides of the marketplace were lined with buildings associated with city government, including sites for meetings of citizens. These meetings of Athenians are seen as the origins of the form of government that is known today as *democracy*.

Ballots and Coins

The archaeologists also found a terracotta box containing six bronze disks. From written sources, they realized that the box was used by juries to give their verdicts in trials. Each member

Conservation

For archaeologists working on the Parthenon, one of the most important tasks is not excavation but restoration. The site and its buildings have suffered badly from centuries of neglect, misuse, and pollution. In 1971 the United Nations Educational, Scientific, and Cultural Organization (UNESCO) warned that the historic ruins were in danger of falling down.

In response, the Greek government set up the Committee for the Preservation of the Acropolis Monuments. The committee hired Manolis Korres as project architect to oversee the restoration work on the Parthenon. Korres is an Athenian who has known the site all his life. His plan was to restore the Parthenon using as many of the original pieces of stone as possible. By studying the color of the blocks of marble lying on the Acropolis, their texture, and even the marks left by the chisels of the original builders, Korres has identified nearly a thousand pieces of stone that were once part of the Parthenon. He plans to put them back in their original places.

Who Owns What?

One of the trickiest issues in archaeology is the ownership of ancient artifacts. Some cases have become the focus of fierce arguments. One example is the Elgin Marbles, a series of marble carvings. They were removed from the Parthenon in Athens by Lord Elgin, the British ambassador, between 1802 and 1812 and are now in London in the British Museum. The Greeks want the marbles back, but the museum says that Elgin bought them legally from the Greek government.

Similar debates are going on around the world. In the past, many museums in Europe and the United States have gotten hold of artifacts from the great civilizations of Egypt, Africa, and other parts of the world. Now the governments of the original countries want them back. They argue that such objects are part of the heritage of their nations and should be returned to them. Many people say that Western archaeologists stole the objects from their rightful owners during a period when Western countries were setting up colonies in Africa and Asia.

Museums and archaeologists often disagree with those arguments. They say that ancient objects do not "belong" to any particular people—especially not in cases where an ancient civilization has died out. Some argue that artifacts can be looked after best in modern museums with money to pay expert curators. They also say that the objects should be on display in cities such as London and Washington, D.C., so that they can be seen by as many international visitors as possible.

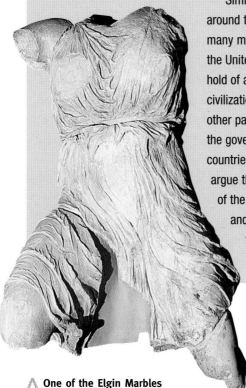

∧ **One of the Elgin Marbles in London.**

of the jury put a bronze disk in the box to show whether they thought the accused person was innocent or guilty. The disks in the box likely indicated freedom or punishment in some forgotten trial.

The agora was also home to the city mint. In its ruins archaeologists found 10 bronze disks ready to be stamped into coins. Many Athenian coins bore the image of an owl, which represented Athena, the goddess of wisdom. The square included a number of stores and taverns, along with *stoas*—ceremonial buildings with porches supported by columns.

Sparta and Athens

The Greeks made no distinction between a city and the rural lands outside its walls. Together they were a *polis*, or city-state. Athens, Corinth,

and Sparta were the largest. Each developed in its own way. The polis of Sparta, for example, focused on physical strength and military training. Spartans voted by pounding on their shields. In Sparta, education focused on producing warriors. Male children were separated from their parents. Brought up with other boys, they were trained to be soldiers.

Sparta's rival, Athens, took a much less warlike approach to education. Paintings on vases and plates show boys in classes learning to give speeches, sing, and play the lyre. Some write on hinged tablets that look a little like the one found in the Uluburun shipwreck. Others write on long rolls of parchment, a kind of paper made from animal skins.

Athena was the goddess of art as well as wisdom, and Athens had a reputation for producing outstanding sculptors and painters. Archaeologists have found thousands of bronze and marble statues of heroes and gods. You can see them in museums in Greece and around the world. The Athenians also honored Athena by painting scenes on pottery and on walls.

Athens at War

Athenians could not ignore military matters altogether. Ancient Greece could be a violent place, and the polis had to be able to defend itself. In the early fifth century B.C., Athens led an

▽ John Camp guides a party around the agora. The Greek word for a marketplace is now used in the term *agoraphobia*, a fear of open spaces.

alliance of Greek states against the fierce Persians. It even cooperated with its rival Sparta.

The massive armies of the Persian kings Darius and Xerxes attacked Greece twice. But they were no match for the better-trained Greek armies. Most of the Persian soldiers were forced to fight and had no interest in

∧ An archaeologist uses a submersible to explore the wreck of a merchant ship in the Aegean Sea.

Greece. The Spartans, Corinthians, and Athenians, on the other hand, were fighting for their freedom. At the great sea battle of Salamis, the Athenian general Themistocles won a decisive victory.

Later in the century, however, the Athenians were at war again with the Spartans and their allies. This long

conflict, called the Peloponnesian Wars, lasted for nearly 30 years and ended in defeat for Athens.

Wooden Walls

In its position at the edge of the sea, Athens depended heavily on its ships. The Athenians would have gone hungry without grain imported by sea, and they trusted their strong navy to protect them. The Athenians called their ships "wooden walls," because they guarded the city against invaders from the sea.

Boats called *triremes*, which had three decks of oars, helped the Athenians beat the Persians. The boats were powered by sails when the wind was up, but more often human muscles sped them through the waves. They were lightweight, easy to turn, and fast—a huge advantage in battle.

The trireme symbolizes Athens itself. Not only did it give the Athenians strength on the seas, but the ordinary men who grasped its oars were citizens of Athens.

Early in the sixth century B.C., a ruler named Solon gave all male citizens the right to vote in an assembly. Solon hoped to revive his country's economy. He gave the vote to

> George Bass examines the ophthalmos, or ship's eye, from a Classical Age wreck in the Aegean Sea.

all free men—rich or poor, landowners or simple workers—and declared that a public assembly would meet three times every month. This was the world's first taste of democracy.

Eye, Eye, Captain

In the summer of 2000, archaeologist George F. Bass and his team explored the remains of a merchant ship that sank in the Aegean Sea during the Classical Age of Greece. It might have been part of the renowned Athenian fleet. The ship had sunk more than 2,400 years before. It was carrying a cargo of wine jugs, bowls, and cups. Amid all these rather common things, divers Sam Lin and Faith Hentschel discovered something amazing: a marble disk, about 6 inches (15 cm) across, resting on the sloping ocean floor. It was what the Greeks called the *ophthalmos*—the ship's eye!

Ancient peoples understood that a ship holds not only its cargo but also the lives of its sailors and passengers. They gave eyes to their ships. Perhaps they believed that the eyes would help the ships find their way.

The marble eye that the divers found had once been painted black, with a pupil and an outer ring to represent the colored iris of the eye, and then attached to the ship's hull with a lead spike. The ophthalmos that Hentschel and Linn found was the first one ever recovered from an ancient wreck.

What happened to the men who sailed on this ship? The wreck did not offer any clues. The sailors were not too far from land when the ship sank. Were they able to swim ashore—or were they dashed against the jagged rocks of the cove? The mystery may never be solved.

Meet an Archaeologist

Dr. Faith Hentschel of Central Connecticut State University has been an underwater archaeologist for more than 30 years. In 2002 she became responsible for organizing INA operations around the world.

◘ What first tweaked your interest in undersea exploration?

◘ My interest in undersea exploration grew from my love of scuba diving. The minute I took my first breath underwater, I knew I wanted to spend as much of my life beneath the sea as possible. When I interviewed with George Bass, the founding father of scientific underwater archaeology, he told me I'd need a Ph.D. in classical archaeology, since I was especially fascinated by the ancient Greeks and Romans. He asked me if I'd ever had any Greek or Latin. I had studied Latin in 7th and 8th grade but did not continue in high school. Clearly, I had a

lot of work to do. Nevertheless, I applied and was accepted into Yale University's Classical Archaeology program. I was also accepted as a field school student on a shipwreck excavation in Turkey. I had found my passion, and I've been following it ever since.

◘ What traits are necessary in an archaeologist, especially an undersea explorer?

◘ Undersea exploration requires a hard-working person with a spirit of adventure and the ability to get along well with other people. Archaeologists live together as a big family, often cut off from the rest of the

world for months at a time, and often in really uncomfortable conditions.

◘ What has been your most exciting expedition so far?

◘ Each expedition has been more exciting than the last, but my favorite was a 3,300-year-old Bronze Age shipwreck—the oldest and deepest ever excavated. We worked for three months for 11 summers, and during every minute on the bottom we were making the most amazing discoveries—such as a gold scarab of the Egyptian queen Nefertiti and the oldest wooden writing tablet in existence. I never wanted to take my wet suit off. This ship carried the culturally richest

ancient cargo ever discovered. It's a time capsule of Late Bronze Age trade in the eastern Mediterranean—one of the most important archaeological discoveries of the 20th century.

🅰 What would you say is an archaeologist's biggest challenge?
🅰 The biggest challenge is that the work is so slow. It has to be. Unless you are prepared to excavate an antiquity or artifact carefully and then have it properly conserved and published, you have simply destroyed a little bit of the past—the exact opposite of what you've set out to do! You'll be amazed to know: The rule of thumb is that for every month of excavation, two years of conservation and research are needed to preserve, evaluate, and analyze—all this before the results can be announced to the world.

🅰 What was the scariest thing that ever happened to you underwater?
🅰 Perhaps the scariest moment was when an unexpected current came up on the surface while my buddies and I were attempting to raise a large ceramic jar from the seabed. We were unable to make headway against the current. The crew on the dinghy saw that we were in distress and came

∧ **Faith Hentschel carries a Bronze Age sword toward the surface.**

with a tow rope for my buddies and the jar, but I was falling farther and farther behind. Finally, they threw me a second line. It was not until I was safely under tow that I snapped a photo.

🅰 What advice would you give to anyone interested in becoming an archaeologist?
🅰 First, I would say that if archaeology is your dream, follow it and never give up. Second, I think the best way to become an archaeologist is simply to be a good student. Some of the most successful archaeologists have begun their studies in completely different fields, but certainly the study of foreign languages is important.

🅰 What is the biggest misconception that people have about archaeology?
🅰 Most people think that archaeologists are looking for treasure or for old things, but what we are really looking for are clues to understanding the human past. Anyone can find old things. Farmers find arrowheads in plowed fields, but that doesn't make them archaeologists. Archaeologists need to preserve and understand what they find, so they can help us understand the past. Also, some people think that archaeologists keep the things they find, but our finds really belong to all the people. We put our treasures into museums for everyone's pleasure and education.

45

Alexander and After

How did Greek culture and ideas survive for so long?

Athena's great city sparkled among the Greek city-states for nearly 200 years, but in 404 B.C., Sparta defeated Athens and tore down its city walls. In the turmoil that followed Athens' defeat, a new power arose. In 338 B.C, King Philip II led Greeks from Macedonia against the Athenians and their allies. Philip won the victory, but two years later, he was killed by an

< An archaeologist examines a handful of coins from a hoard found at the town of Aphrodisias, which passed from Greek to Roman control.

HELLENISTIC PERIOD
circa 323 - 31 B.C.

B.C. 0 A.D.

| 1000 | 500 | 100 |

assassin. His son Alexander created an even bigger empire and earned himself the name by which he is still known: Alexander the Great.

Greek Culture Spreads

Under Alexander, Greek culture changed and spread as his armies carried out bold campaigns of conquest. This new kind of culture— known as Hellenistic, meaning "from Greece"—spread through northern Africa and west and central Asia. Its influence reached Libya, Iran, Iraq, Pakistan, Afghanistan, and Egypt. Greek gods appear with local gods on coins found as far away as India. Alexander founded many cities. In Egypt he named a new city after himself—Alexandria.

Let There Be Light!

When Alexander died, one of his top generals became pharaoh of Egypt and took the name Ptolemy Soter. In 290 B.C, Ptolemy began building an amazing structure at Pharos in Alexandria's harbor. It was the world's first lighthouse. At about 450 feet (137 m) high, it was the second tallest building in existence. Only the 50-story Great Pyramid at Giza in Egypt was taller.

By the time the Pharos Lighthouse was finished, Ptolemy's son, Ptolemy II, had come to the throne. The lighthouse designer, Sostrates, was proud of his work and wanted to carve his name on the foundation stone. Ptolemy II insisted that his own name should be carved there instead. Sostrates knew better than to argue with the pharaoh, but he was clever—and sneaky. Sostrates carved his own name on the

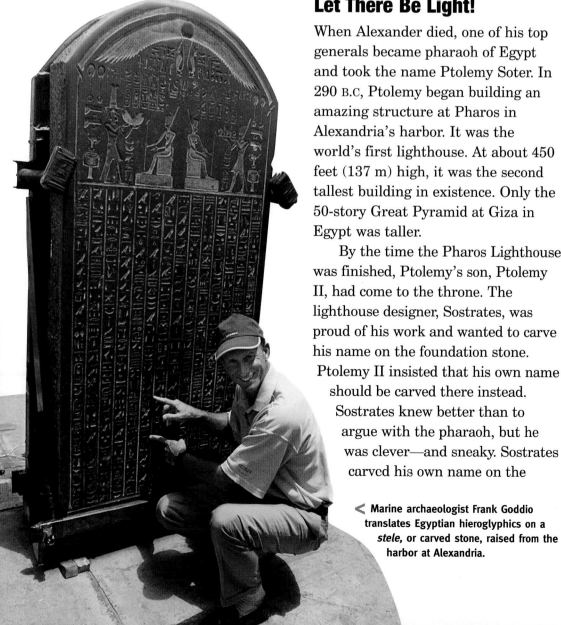

< Marine archaeologist Frank Goddio translates Egyptian hieroglyphics on a *stele,* or carved stone, raised from the harbor at Alexandria.

> A curator makes a final adjustment to a 2,000-year-old granite bust found on the bed of the harbor at Alexandria.

V The lighthouse or Pharos of Alexandria was one of the wonders of the ancient world. Fuel for the fire on top was carried up through a vent in the center of the building. This drawing is an artist's impression—no one knows exactly what the building really looked like.

< This giant burial mound at Vergina in Macedonia in northern Greece has been half excavated. One of its tombs contained the remains of Philip II of Macedon, the father of Alexander the Great.

stone, then covered it with plaster. In the plaster, he carved Ptolemy's name. Over time, the plaster fell away, leaving the designer's name for all to see—just as Sostrates had planned.

The Pharos Lighthouse was built with massive marble blocks. The bottom level was shaped like a huge box. Above it rose an eight-sided tower topped by an open-sided dome. A fire

burning inside the dome led ships safely into the harbor. Ancient writers reported that the dome's curved mirror could reflect light up to 100 miles (160 km) away. Some claimed that the Egyptians used it as a weapon to concentrate light and burn their enemies' ships. That is unlikely, however. Modern scientists were not able to produce such a powerful beam

of light until after the invention of the laser in 1960!

Light in the Sea

The lighthouse stood for centuries after the Greeks and the Ptolemies had gone. But earthquakes weakened it, and it collapsed in A.D. 1326. The great Pharos Lighthouse—one of the Seven Wonders of the World—was gone. But not forever.

In 1994, scuba-diving archaeologists began a search for the remains of the famous lighthouse. They placed markers on underwater blocks of stone in Alexandria harbor so that an Electronic Distance Measurement station on shore could map their exact positions. Adding information gathered by global positioning satellites, they fed all the data into a computer.

A Conqueror's Bones

In 1977 excavators led by Manolis Andronicus unearthed a massive tomb in Vergina. Inside they discovered a bronze lantern and box-shaped coffin decorated with a Macedonian star. When they opened the coffin, they found charred human remains, a skull, and a still-beautiful wreath of golden oak leaves and acorns. They had found the tomb of Philip II of Macedon!

Coin from the reign of Philip II

Scientists and archaeologists are still exploring the harbor floor, and will for a long time to come. They have found remnants of many different buildings embedded in the ocean floor,

< Every Macedonian royal tomb experts have found has been looted—except that of King Philip II. Finds like this gold chest suggest what great treasures may have been lost to the grave-robbers.

∧ **This huge sculpture stood at the Temple of Aphrodite in Aphrodisias.**

plus statues, sphinxes, and ancient columns—an underwater paradise for history lovers.

Goodbye Greece, Hello Rome

While the Ptolemies ruled in Egypt, Alexander's empire in the east broke into separate kingdoms. Near the Meander River in Turkey, Kenan Erim from New York University began excavating a Hellenistic city at Aphrodisias in 1961. He found many traces of a city founded in the second century B.C., when an agora, or marketplace, had been built. The site was already old, however. The city's theater had been built into the side of a mound that marked the site of an older settlement. And the city's shrine to the goddess Aphrodite had once stood in open countryside.

The archaeologists found a second marketplace near the first one. It had an ornamental pool in the center. They believe that the pool may have been intended to prevent the area from being used for public meetings, like marketplaces in Greece.

The building of the pool reflected the arrival of a new power that did not encourage democracy. A new temple built in the city between 30 and 20 B.C. is carved with the name of its builder,

> Archaeologists use a surveying instrument called a *theodolite* to take measurements of the stadium at Aphrodisias.

< Kenan Erim carefully cleans a marble head found during excavations of the theater at Aphrodisias.

a Roman. Beginning in the second century B.C., Rome gradually took over virtually all of Alexander's former empire, including Athens itself.

Many Roman leaders appreciated Greek culture. They wanted to use it to hold together the different peoples of the lands they conquered. Under Roman rule, Aphrodisias thrived. The emperor Augustus called it "the one city from all of Asia that I have selected to call my own." The city was famed for its marble quarries—and for the local sculptures that preserved echoes in stone of its Greek past.

Rescuing the Past

CHAPTER 6

Is there anything left to learn about the ancient Greeks?

We know more about the Greeks than about most other ancient peoples. You might think that archaeologists have learned almost everything they can about ancient Greece. But you'd be wrong. Excavations go on all the time, and every one of them might yield a fascinating new glimpse into the past. Just when the experts think they have solved one mystery about how the Greeks lived, another one appears. More than a century after Heinrich Schliemann found Troy, fabled sites are still being explored—and

< Although new discoveries are constantly being made, archaeologists also make sure that sites like this temple on the Acropolis in Athens are carefully preserved.

more await discovery. One of the most famous Greek heroes who fought at Troy, for example, was Odysseus. Homer said that the mighty warrior was the king of Ithaca. There is still a Greek island named Ithaki—but it does not resemble the island that Homer described. For one thing, it is in the wrong place.

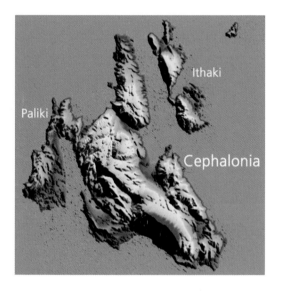

∧ This satellite image shows the sites of Paliki and modern Ithaki.

Everyone assumed that Homer was wrong about Ithaca. In 1998, however, Robert Bittlestone decided, like Schliemann, to follow the poet's clues. He studied satellite images of the Greek islands and records of geological activity. He came to two remarkable conclusions: that Homer's Ithaca is not modern Ithaki and that Ithaca-of-old is no longer an island. Geologic activity has raised the seabed to join Ithaca to the tourist island of Cephalonia, as the Paliki peninsula.

Bittlestone's team planned to call on experts in geology, microbiology, and sea levels to confirm his theory that Paliki is Ithaca-of-old. But the team are already convinced. They believe they have found the site of Odysseus's palace. By the expedition's end in 2012, the team hope to have learned many more secrets about Homer's Ithaca.

Destroyed by the Gods

Other sites are also yielding new finds. In 2001 a team led by Steven Soter and Dora Katsonopoulou found Helike in Achaea in southern Greece. The city was the site of a famous sanctuary to Helikonian Poseidon, god of earthquakes and the sea.

In 373 B.C. the city was destroyed by an earthquake and a tsunami. The team found walls, coins, and other remains from the old city. But they also found a bigger surprise: an early Bronze Age city on the same site. The first Helike had suffered the same fate as its successor. It was submerged about 2,000 years earlier.

Surprises on Salamis

Another investigation, led by Yannos Lolos, explored a cave on the island of Salamis. Lolos found a fragment of a clay cup from the fifth century B.C. The cup was marked with six letters: EURIPI. Salamis had been home to one of ancient Greece's most famous playwrights. Some of his 92 plays are still performed. Greek and Roman

writers reported that he used to write in a cave. The playwright's name was Euripides. Lolos had found the retreat of one of the most famous Greeks of all.

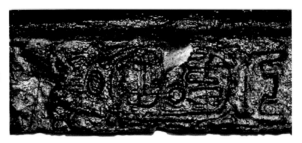

∧ This piece of bronze armor from Salamis is stamped with the royal mark of Ramses II.

For Lolos, that was not the end of Salamis's treasures. In 2006 Lolos announced another find: an ancient palace built during the Mycenean period. Lolos found a piece of armor stamped with the mark of Pharaoh Ramses II of Egypt, which helped date the site to the 13th century B.C. Lolos believes he has found the palace of Ajax, a legendary warrior who, according to Homer, fought in the Trojan War. Yet again, archaeology connects in a wonderful way with legends that few people had taken seriously. How many other Greek legends might turn out to contain more than a little truth?

∨ This hilltop palace on Salamis had 33 rooms and may have belonged to the mighty warrior Ajax.

The Years Ahead

There are still many discoveries to be made in Greece. They may help clarify literary sources, or they may reveal more surprises about the Dark Age. Underwater archaeology, in particular, promises to yield great treasures. A new project lets archaeologists use remote-controlled underwater vehicles to reach archaeological sites at depths that are too great for divers to work at easily.

Archaeology in Greece is not only about making discoveries. It is also about what happens afterward. The country's ruins and artifacts help attract 12 million tourists a year. The Greeks are planning ways to make sure visitors have access to the historical sites without damaging them or changing their nature. Conservation is an important part of archaeology.

Meanwhile, work goes on at the Acropolis in Athens. The buildings have been damaged by erosion and neglect. The polluted air in Athens includes chemicals that eat into the stone of the building.

Today, many Greek experts are campaigning to get back treasures that were removed by archaeologists in the past. Governments and police everywhere are also cracking down on looting—the unauthorized removal of artifacts by art dealers and smugglers.

V The Elgin Marbles will not stay in the British Museum if many Greek experts have their way. They will be returned to a new museum in Greece.

Glossary

aristocrats – members of the noble class of society

artifact – any object changed by human activity

Bronze Age – a period from around the 17th to the 12th centuries B.C., when the Greeks made vessels and weapons from bronze

cemeteries – places where a number of dead bodies are buried

ceramic – made from clay

circa – about; used to indicate a date that is approximate, and abbreviated as ca

colonies – settlements set up by cities or countries in other lands; colonies are ruled by the cities or powers that establish them

conservation – archaeological work that aims to protect ancient objects or buildings from further damage

democracy – a system of government in which all members of society have an equal say, usually by voting for people to represent them in the body that runs the society

ebony – a valuable dark wood

excavation – an archaeological dig

global positioning satellites – a system of satellites in orbit around the Earth that can measure the accurate location of objects on Earth

hieroglyphics – a system of writing with pictures developed by the Egyptians

legendary – relating to a story that is well known but probably only partly true, or perhaps not true at all

lighthouse – a tall building with a light on top to warn ships away from dangerous rocks

lyre – a stringed musical instrument shaped like a harp

magnetometers – instruments for measuring the Earth's magnetic field

nautical – relating to sailors or ships

playwright – a person who writes plays

pollution – exhaust fumes, smoke, and other substances that make the air or water dirty

resin – a substance formed by hardened sap that leaks from trees

restoration – the process of repairing old objects to bring them as close as possible to their original state

sacrifice – an offering to the gods, often involving the ritual killing of an animal

scarab – a lucky charm in the shape of a beetle

scuba – equipment that lets divers breathe underwater; the word comes from the initials of *S*elf-*C*ontained *U*nderwater *B*reathing *A*pparatus

sculptor – a person who carves stone

sources – all of the material from which archeologists learn information, such as written documents, old objects, and excavated ruins

sphinxes – Egyptian statues with lion's bodies and human heads

stronghold – a defended site, such as a fortress

terra-cotta – a brownish-red clay for pottery

tomb painting – Egyptian art made to decorate burial chambers

Bibliography

Books

Greece: Temples, Tombs, and Treasures (Lost Civilizations). Alexandria, VA: Time-Life Books, 1998.

Pomeroy, Sarah, et al. *A Brief History of Ancient Greece: Politics, Society, and Culture.* New York: Oxford University Press, 2004.

Whitley, James R., et al. *The Archaeology of Ancient Greece* (Cambridge World Archaeology). New York: Cambridge University Press, 2001.

Wondrous Realms of the Aegean (Lost Civilizations). Alexandria, VA: Time-Life Books, 1993.

Articles

Alexander, Caroline. "Alexander the Conqueror." NATIONAL GEOGRAPHIC (March 2000): 42–75.

Bass, George F. "Golden Age Treasures." NATIONAL GEOGRAPHIC (March 2003): 102–117.

Bass, George F. "Oldest Known Shipwreck Reveals Splendors of the Bronze Age." NATIONAL GEOGRAPHIC (December 1987): 692–733.

Gore, Rick. "When the Greeks Went West." NATIONAL GEOGRAPHIC (November 1994): 4–37.

Severin, Tim. "The Quest for Ulysses." NATIONAL GEOGRAPHIC (August 1986): 196–225.

Further Reading

Column, Padraic. *The Children's Homer: The Adventures of Odysseus and the Tale of Troy.* New York: Aladdin Paperbacks, 2004.

Eyewitness Ancient Greece. New York: Dorling Kindersley, 2004.

Powell, Anton, and Sean Sheehan. *Ancient Greece* (Cultural Atlas for Young People). New York: Facts on File, 2003.

Web Sites

AOL TeacherNet Ancient Greece
http://home.aol.com/TeacherNet/AncientGreece.html

BBC Schools guide to Ancient Greece
http://www.bbc.co.uk/schools/ancientgreece/index.shtml

History for Kids Ancient Greece index
http://www.historyforkids.org/learn/greeks/

UNESCO World Heritage List for Greece
http://whc.unesco.org/en/statesparties/gr

Index

Boldface indicates illustrations.

About the Author

MARNI McGEE grew up in North Carolina. She is a graduate of the University of North Carolina at Chapel Hill and has an M.A. in religion from Yale Divinity School.

Ms. McGee is the author of 11 published books. Her career as a children's book writer began as entertainment for her own children. McGee has had a number of jobs, but claims only one profession: "Writing for children is the highest honor and privilege that I can imagine. Children are worth the very best we can give them." This is her first book for National Geographic.

About the Consultant

MICHAEL SHANKS is an archaeologist, author, and educator. From 1993 to 1998 he was head of archaeology at the University of Wales, Lampeter. Currently at California's Stanford University, he is a professor of classical archaeology and Stanford's Hoskins Scholar.

Λ Gold-plated Mycenaean wooden box from
the second half of the 16th century B.C.

Author Dedication

In memory of Dick Tener, who loved Greece and lived with exuberance, generosity, and joy.

One of the world's largest nonprofit
scientific and educational organizations, the
National Geographic Society was founded in
1888 "for the increase and diffusion of
geographic knowledge." Fulfilling this
mission, the Society educates and inspires millions
every day through its magazines, books, television
programs, videos, maps and atlases, research grants,
the National Geographic Bee, teacher workshops, and
innovative classroom materials. The Society is
supported through membership dues, charitable gifts,
and income from the sale of its educational products.
This support is vital to National Geographic's mission
to increase global understanding and promote
conservation of our planet through exploration,
research, and education.

For more information, please call 1-800-NGS-LINE
(647-5463) or write to the following address:

National Geographic Society
1145 17th Street N.W.
Washington, D.C. 20036-4688
U.S.A.

Visit the Society's Web site:
www.nationalgeographic.com

Library of Congress Cataloging-in-Publication Data
available upon request
Hardcover ISBN-10: 0-7922-7826-7
        ISBN-13: 978-0-7922-7826-9
Library Edition ISBN-10: 0-7922-7872-0
        ISBN-13: 978-0-7922-7872-6

Printed in Mexico

Series design by Jim Hiscott
The body text is set in Century Schoolbook
The display text is set in Helvetica Neue, Clarendon

National Geographic Society

John M. Fahey, Jr., *President and Chief Executive
Officer;* Gilbert M. Grosvenor, *Chairman of the Board;*
Nina D. Hoffman, *Executive Vice President, President of
Books Publishing Group*

Staff for This Book

Nancy Laties Feresten, *Vice President, Editor-in-Chief
of Children's Books*
Virginia Ann Koeth, *Project Editor*
Bea Jackson, *Director of Design and Illustration*
David Seager, *Art Director*
Lori Epstein, Greta Arnold, National Geographic Image
Sales, *Illustrations Editors*
Jean Cantu, *Illustrations Specialist*

Carl Mehler, *Director of Maps*
Priyanka Lamichhane, *Assistant Editor*
R. Gary Colbert, *Production Director*
Lewis R. Bassford, *Production Manager*
Vincent P. Ryan, Maryclare Tracy, *Manufacturing
Managers*

For the Brown Reference Group, plc

Tim Cooke, *Managing Editor*
Alan Gooch, *Book Designer*
Becky Cox, *Picture Research*

Photo Credits

Front cover: © Archivo Iconografico, S.A./Corbis
Spine: © Gordon Gahan/ Getty Images
Back cover: Background image: gds/sefa/Corbis; Coin: ©
Bibliotheque Nationale, Paris, France/Snark/Art
Resource NY
Icon: © Mike Lui/Shutterstock

NGIC = National Geographic Image Collection
1, © Bibliotheque Nationale, Paris, France/Snark Art
Resource, NY; 2-3, © Kevin Fleming/NGIC; 4, ©
Jonathan Blair/NGIC; 6, © Gordan Gahan/NGIC/Getty
Images; 9, © Michael Shanks; 10, © AKG Images; 11,
© Acropolis Museum/Werner Forman Archive; 12-13,
© Bill Curtsinger/NGIC; 14, © Bill Curtsinger/NGIC;
15 top, © Bill Curtsinger/NGIC; 15 bottom, © Bill
Curtsinger/NGIC; 16, © Bill Curtsinger/NGIC; 17 top,
© Bill Curtsinger/NGIC; 17 bottom, © Bill Curtsinger/
NGIC; 18-19, © Rosalie Seidler/NGIC; 20, © William
(Maryland) Cook/NGIC; 21, © Randy Olsen/NGIC; 22
top, © AKG Images; 22 bottom; © AKG Images; 23,
© Warner Bros./Alex Bailey/The Kobal Collection; 24-
25, © James L. Stanfield/NGIC; 26, © Gordan Gahan/
NGIC; 27, © James L. Stanfield/NGIC; 28, © Gianni
Dagli Orti/Corbis; 29, © James L. Stanfield/NGIC; 30-
31, © Roger Wood/Corbis; 32, © The Art Archive/
Corbis; 33, © James P. Blair/NGIC; 34, © Sisse
Brimberg/NGIC; 35, © Roger Wood/Corbis; 36-37, ©
Petros Giannakouris/AP/Empics; 38, © Werner Forman
Archives; 40, © British Museum, London/Werner
Forman Archive; 41, © Mrs Mary G. Smith/NGIC; 42,
© Courtney Platt/NGIC; 43, © Courtney Platt/NGIC;
44, © Faith Hentschel; 45, © Don Frey/NGIC; 46-47,
© Jonathan Blair/Corbis; 48, © Reuters/Corbis; 49 top,
© Kirsty Wigglesworth/ PA/Empics; 49 bottom,
© Private Collection/Archives Charmet/The Bridgeman
Art Library; 50, © Gordan Gahan/NGIC; 51 top, ©
Private Collection/The Bridgeman Art Library; 51
bottom, © Gianni Dagli Orti/Corbis; 52, © Richard
Hamilton Smith/Corbis; 53 top, © Jonathan Blair/
Corbis; 53 bottom, © Jonathan Blair/Corbis; 54-55,
© James P. Blair/NGIC; 56, © Originated by Robert
Brittlestone from Hellenic Military Geographic Service;
57 top, © AP/Empics; 57 bottom, © AP/Empics; 58,
© British Museum, London/Werner Forman Archive;
63, © AKG Images.

Front cover: Sculpture of the head of a warrior
from the temple of Aphaia in Aegina
Page 1 and back cover: An Athenian drachme.
The owl was the symbol of both Athens and the
goddess Athena.
Pages 2–3: A ship sails past the ruins of the Temple
of Poseidon at Cape Sounion, Greece.

NATIONAL GEOGRAPHIC I
EOGRAPHIC INVESTIGAGE
INVESTIGATES NATIONAL
ES NATIONAL GEOGRAPH
L GEOGRAPHIC INVESTIGA
IC INVESTIGATES NATION
ATES NATIONAL GEOGRAP
NAL GEOGRAPHIC INVEST
PHIC INVESTIGATES NATI
GATES NATIONAL GEOGR
ONAL GEOGRAPHIC INVES
RAPHIC INVESTIGATES NA
STIGATES NATIONAL GEO
ATIONAL GEOGRAPHIC IN
OGRAPHIC INVESTIGATES
NVESTIGATES NATIONAL
S NATIONAL GEOGRAPHIC